Home Organizing

Quick Guide on How to Clean, Declutter and Organize Your Room

Lisa McCall

Contents

Introduction

There is a common say that east or west home is best however what are some of the feelings that comes to your mind whenever you get to your home; does your home make your heart rejoice or sink? As much as many people spend most of their time outside the home than they do at home; home should be a place that fills one with comfort and peace of mind. There is nothing that ignites those positive emotions that we desire to have like walking into your home with the knowledge that it's well organized, clean and free of any clutter.

Being in a home with endless piles of laundry that require attention alongside other to dos can be so exhausting and overwhelming. When a home is filled with clutter and other activities that demand attention then there are higher chances of one getting stress and depression. Being in an organized home generally impacts every aspect of one's life positively. Preparing food in a kitchen that's sparkling clean with spotless countertops only help in enhancing once desire to eat better.

Many relationships have been ruined due to the inability of sustaining a well organized and clean home. Organizing the home alone is not enough; one has to develop a mechanism of sustaining the well organized home by having routines for cleaning and decluttering. **Home organizing: Quick Guide on How to Clean, Declutter and Organize Your Room** is a book that has shared in detail some of the things that one need to do in order to effectively manage clutter and organize the homes well. This book has shared various topics in depth such as how you can organize every space within the home, organization tips for small homes, how to declutter room by room, before you buy tips, and natural cleaning products amongst others.

It's one thing to learn how to organize and declutter your home and another thing to implement what has been read. I encourage you to read this book all through to the end and get valuable insight that you can implement and take advantage of for a well organized home. Whether you are living in a large compound or just having a small house; the information shared in this book will equip you will strategies that you can use to organize your home without having to feel overwhelmed due to the size of the home and the mess there in.

Each chapter in this guide has actionable steps that you can take including the steps you can use to prepare natural cleaning products. Take your time and read it all through to the end as you may not be aware of that insight that will be capable of transforming your home.

Congratulations and enjoy your reading!

Chapter 1

Home Organization

It's a delighting thing to be in a home that's well organized and clean as it comes with some level of comfort and peace of mind. A well organized home that's clean and free of any forms of clutter is not only relaxing to be in but also quite comfortable. The daily cares of life and the routines normally make it difficult for quite a number of people to organize and clean their homes. Organizing and cleaning your home can in a great way make your life easier and less stressful. If you intend to leave a happier and comfortable life in your home then you should commit to organizing your home and ensuring it's clean and free of clutter.

With a well organized and cleaned home, you don't have to spend a lot of time locating things within the home. You will actually be aware of where to look into for specific things and that also saves time. A well organized home is also aesthetically pleasing and comes with a lot of confidence especially when guests appear without having any prior information. This guide provides actionable strategies that you can use to organize and declutter your home for a more comfortable and fulfilling life.

How to organize every space within the home

Different areas within the home are used for different types of tasks and knowing how each space can be organized is vital if one is to have a home that's well organized and free of all manner of clutter. Organizing the home can be a constant struggle for those who lack sufficient insight on how o go through the process. If you lack knowledge on how to organize your home then you will always find yourself at the edge as you work hard to tweak systems and get rid of clutter that never seem to get cleared.

Here are some of the ways that you can use to organize and clean your home;

Take everything out

Begin by clearing out the entire space by getting things out so that you can clearly evaluate the space that you have available. Starting organizing your room when all the space is blank helps as you can be clearer on where to place some things.

Purge unnecessary things

Once you have removed all the things out of their space, take time and purge out the things that are not necessary. If there are some items that you no longer use that are lying idle in your room then you can purge them out and pack them into a trash bag for disposal. One thing that makes the house to look cluttered most of the times is keeping items that we no longer use within the house. You need to be seriously ruthless and only keep the things you feel that you must have.

You can either throw the items away or donate it to someone who may still find it to be valuable. The more you get rid of the unnecessary materials within your room, the less cluttered the room will be. Once you have purged the unnecessary items that you don't need then you will be left with more space within the room that you can use to arrange and pack your items in.

Put like items together

Once you have purged the items that you don't need, then you need to group the like items together. If you are organizing your kitchen you need to place similar spices together, the similar kitchen utensils together, canned foods, baking items and such like. If you group items that are alike together then picking them up whenever you want to use them becomes much easier. You can also know easily when one item is getting out of stock so that you can restock.

You can also group the items according to category. Instead of disposing the boxes that you have available in your house, you can instead use them to pack different categories of like items. For example, you can have all the canned foods packed into one container and another container can also be packed with other items that are of a similar category. It helps in minimizing the space utilized for storage and reducing clutter.

You can even go ahead and label the bins so that you don't end up mixing the items up whenever you are picking them out. Make use of items such as paper clips, rubber bands, glue and dry erase markers to help you with organizing and packaging the items. Once you have placed the items into the appropriate category then ensure that you go ahead and label the tins. Labeling will help you with determining where every item is placed.

You can either choose to use a printed tag for labeling your box or can that you have used for packing the items. You can also create your own labels and use to label the tins. Alongside the label, you can also write the items that are placed in the can on the label for easier reference.

Refill your Space

Once you have separated and labeled the items, then the next step is to ensure that you fill the available space by arranging things accordingly. Put the items back into the respective spaces. Place the items that you use most in an accessible spot then fill the remaining gaps with other items in order of how frequent you use them.

Train yourself to put things in their rightful place once you have used them. Once you have arranged everything into its spot; the only way to keep them in the spot is by ensuring that everything has a specific spot. You have to put more effort and develop the habit of ensuring that things are in their rightful place after you have used them. If you go back to your former way of doing things then you shall have done zero work as it will just be a matter of time before things are back to their messy state.

Be flexible to change

Maintaining your home in an organized and clean way will require you to make a few tweaks on how you handle things within the home. You will need to change how you manage items such as clothes, how you sort the dirty ones for laundry, how you dispose of used items that are not required. You should therefore be flexible and embrace the new way of doing things if your home is to remain well organized. If your system of organizing things makes it difficult for you to retrieve things whenever you require them then you can work on replacing them with more flexible ones.

For example, Instead of having all your clothes packed together in a suitcase, you can organize for drawers and a wardrobe where you can easily pull the ones you want without messing with the rest of the clothes. Instead of using boxes to store stuff, you can also opt for drawers that you can just pull and retrieve whatever you want to use. Never be afraid of replacing your system of arranging the home with something that's more flexible and working. Remember that different areas within the house require different type of bins, dividers or even shelving of proper organization of the room is to be maintained.

To succeed in organizing your home, take your time and concentrate in one room at a time. Focusing in getting the entire home organized in a few days can be quite overwhelming and may deny you the motivation that you need to organize your home.

How to create more storage space

The reason why most homes stay cluttered and disorganized is due to the fact that many people have a lot of stuff that doesn't fit well in the spaces that they have available. To organize your home in an effective way, you need to learn how to utilize the space that you have available within the home. To get sufficient space within you home; you have to engage in the following;

Learn how to declutter

Clutter has a way of draining energy while and also costs time and money to keep up with. If you are to maximize storage space within your home then you to engage in decluttering your home regularly. Declutter your home by moving from one room to another and if in case the rooms are large and filled with stuff then you have to start by breaking them up into small zones or portions. You need to work much faster and get to decide on the items that you need to toss and those that you need to keep. You can then donate or even trash the items you are disposing.

Find the best storage solutions

Once you have sorted the items in the room you should then look out for the best storage solution that fits your needs. A good storage solution should be able to accomplish the following;

- Help in creating more space
- Should help in streamlining your organization by grouping the like items together.
- Should make finding the items much easier by creating a well organized and proper home.

There are different types of storage materials that you can opt for such as clear plastic containers, drawers and even boxes.

Maximize the prime space for storage

Your prime storage space is the space that you have available between your knees and the shoulders. This is the space that is easiest to reach and the rule of out of sight out of mind applies when identifying your prime storage space. Remember to store the things that you frequently use in the prime storage space. You need to think of the things that you reach out for most of the times then store them in the space where you can easily pick them out. F you want something to be easily available for use then you need to store it where you can still see it.

Think vertically

Majority of the people think from left to right or right to left however you should also not ignore the space that's above your head and beneath your feet. If you are to take advantage of the higher spaces then you should invest in a good ladder that allows you to reach the upper areas comfortably. Remember not to store something that's too heavy above your head.

Plastic containers can be utilized for storing things near the floor as they make everything easy to find.

Choose the right storage for your space

Before you buy the plastic containers and other storage items, ensure that they can fit well in your space. It can be more frustrating when you carry the items home only to realize that the containers cannot fit well in the drawers you intend to store them in or even in the fridge and other available spaces. If you have doubt about the ideal storage items to purchase then you can even go ahead and take measurements so that you are sure of the available that the storage is capable of fitting well in the space available.

As we shared earlier, ensure that you label the storage items for easy retrieval. Use of labels also helps in giving the home such a professional and polished look.

Make use of offsite storage

It's important that you first organize your storage spaces before you organize your living space. Organizing your storage space will enable you to take advantage of as much space that's available as possible. If you have a ton of some extra items that are crammed into your kitchen then you can organize some storage space in your basement or a free closet that you could be having available in your home. Offsite storage is quite ideal if you have a lot of items to store especially if you intend to host an estate sale.

Small home organization tips

Clutter can be a constant thing to deal with especially if you are living in small spaces however you can still get more organized with the small space that you could be having available. The following tips can be used to make the small home spaces more organized and uncluttered. Take advantage of these creative storage solutions for a well organized home.

Small kitchen space storage

- Mix the open shelves with less bulky ones that keep the items mostly used much closer.
- Install appliances such as microwaves and fridges into your cabinetry so that the countertop and floor can be cleared.
- Store countertop items into containers and trays.

Small bedroom space storage

- If the room also doubles as the living room then choose a bed that can be hidden when not in use.
- You can also install a built in wall unit that's fixed with nigh table trays or just mount floating shelves at the level of the bed that you can use for holding an alarm clock or a reading lamp.
- You can use a ladder or a tote to store some of the spare items such as linen in style.
- Maximize the unseen space with zippered soft chests that can be kept right under the bed.

Small living room space storage

- Make use of the available TV space and the cabinetry by spreading your entertainment unit from wall to wall.
- You can also combine function and comfort with use of an upholstered storage ottoman.
- To create a visually cohesive outlook that's appealing and less cluttered; try to keep similar items together such as having floor cushions stacked in one place and board games beneath the table.

- Make good use of the wall space without having to sacrifice style. You can fix a shelf then conceal it with a stack of books.

Small bathroom space storage

- You can maximize the vertical space by placing some linen tower above the toilet or at the corner.
- Keep your bathroom supplies nearby in plastic container or some spa like woven basket.
- Clear up the cabinet and the counter space by mounting the magnifying mirror to the wall.

Chapter 2

Decluttering Room by Room

As much as we have tackled how to organize and arrange your home; managing clutter is another important aspect that require proper attention if the homes are to stay well organized and clean. There are millions of households that are leaving in cluttered homes with many feeling overwhelmed with how they can manage the clutter that seems to be getting out of control each day. Clutter is destructive and if not well managed on a regular basis, there are higher chances that the clutter ay spiral into unmanageable heights.

What is decluttering?

Decluttering is removing stuff or items that you don't need in your home. Many people confuse decluttering with organizing or storing stuff, however decluttering entails removing the stuff that you don't need but are filling space within the home. For a home to be well organized, items needs to be sorted out and assessed carefully so that only the required items are left in the home. Many people complain of not having sufficient space in their homes for doing valuable tasks like creating a home office space however such can be realized with proper organization and decluttering of the home.

There are simple steps that can help with clearing clutter and being able to maintain a well organized and clean home. Decluttering the home is such a big job and can be overwhelming if not keenly looked into. The best way to tackle clutter is by focusing on one room at a time or even a space within the room. For example instead of focusing in decluttering the entire kitchen; you can instead focus on the kitchen cabinets then move to the next space or zone within the kitchen until the entire room is decluttered.

To declutter your home effectively; you don't have to use some fancy tools all that you may require are just 5 baskets, bins or empty boxes. You should set the bins in place before you start de-cluttering the rooms. You can then put the bins into different categories such as;

Put away: The first bin can be used for the items you intend to put away. This are items that might have crept to your storage spaces and may include things like having a sweat shirt in the kitchen, a cup or mop in the bedroom and such like.

Recycle: The next bin can be used for putting items that you intend to recycle like the papers, plastic containers or glass containers.

Fix/Mend: This bin can be used for items that require tinkering. You can place things like nice items that you still value but require some fixing.

Trash: This bin is for putting items that are to be trashed.

Donate: You can place items that you are willing to donate to another person or o a charitable organization.

Here are some of the steps you can follow when decluttering specific rooms

Bathrooms

When decluttering the bathrooms you can begin with the medicine cabinet. Take out everything then discard the outdated make up, skin care and medication. Put everything that you need back into the cabinet then keep those that you frequently use at a closer reach where you can easily pick them. You can then move on to the drawers. Remove all the items then carry out an evaluation of the things that you are keeping and those you are tossing away.

Return those items you are still using back to the drawers with those frequently used on top of the drawer. You can repeat the same routine with the tub or shower. Pull all the items from below your bathroom sink then declutter them.

Bedrooms

Begin by making your bed and removing everything on the night stand that shouldn't be there then place in the put away bin. These may include the books that you have already read, the pens and papers, the broken eye glasses and other items that should be kept away. You can then trash or recycle the items that you no longer use accordingly. You can repeat the same routine with your dressers and go through each of the drawers in your bedroom and pull out clothes that you no longer wear. You can then donate the clothes that you don't need alongside other items in your bedroom.

Consider recycling or tossing away any item that you may not have used for over a year or even six months. You can then rearrange your bedroom and return items to their respective places.

Closet and clothing

One of the easiest ways you can use to declutter your closet is to declutter the clothing according to type. You can begin with the shoes, boots, dresses according to type then denim amongst others. If you are looking to your collection of jeans then you can decide on the type to toss away or donate. You can repeat the same process with other clothing collection as you decide on what to keep and those to toss.

Once you have gone through the entire closet then you will have about four piles of items to deal with. You will need to put away the clothing and other items in wrong spot. If in case you found socks in your closet then you can return them to your dresser. The dirty laundry can be put to the hamper then taken to the laundry room. Any clothing that requires repair can be taken to the tailor or dry cleaning for those that require dry cleaning

Foyers, entryways and mudrooms

As much as you may not have foyer or mudroom, most homes have an entry way and regardless of how small it may be de-cluttering it can help with making it to be more functional. You can begin the process of de-cluttering with the side tables, desk or console. Go through each of the drawers and remove the contents then decide faster on what to toss recycle or keep. Go over each of the drawers and the desk tops then categorize the items accordingly.

The entire closet should be decluttered just like any other space with the items placed in the right categories. The entry is one place that normally picks a lot of clutter that comes from other rooms. You will need to spend more time in putting away items that need t be put away.

Kitchen

Keeping the kitchen free of clutter can be quite a challenge however it's possible to have a clean and well organized kitchen that's free of any clutter. Most of the times are spent in the kitchen cooking, eating and even socializing so it's possible to find items in the kitchen that should not be there in the first place. To declutter the kitchen, you need to focus on one type of item each time like the utensils, bake ware, glassware, and cutting boards.

Begin by emptying the space and assessing each item then sorting them in accordance with what needs to be put away, trashed or even donated. Start with the storage spaces like the pantry and the upper cabinet's then move to the drawers and the countertops. Remove as many items as possible off the countertops and into the storage spaces. You should only keep the things that you use each day on the counter tops.

Living room

The living room is one of those rooms in the house that require consistent decluttering if it's to remain organized and tidy. This is because it's one of the mostly used rooms in the house. To declutter the living room, you need to decide on permanent storage spaces that you can use for storing the commonly used items such as the remote controls, the books and the magazines. You should also commit to decluttering the living room regularly if it's to stay tidy.

Begin by de-cluttering the bookcases, the side tables and console then move to the coffee table and the entertainment area. Empty the places then assess the items that are stored in the space. Put away things that need to be away from the living room as you also de-clutter the area around the television and home theatre. You can then store items such as chargers, gaming equipment and gadgets in places where you can easily find and use them.

If you keep toys in the living room then you can also asses them for wear and tear and remove any clutter that could be amongst the toys. You can also dispose or donate the toys that your kids are no longer using.

Once you have sorted out the items according to each room, ensure that put away the items to specific rooms that they belong in. You can also go ahead and trash those items that need to be trashed and store those that should be stored.

How to stop clutter before it piles

Maintaining a well organized home require a lot of discipline and commitment to cleanliness and doing away with clutter.

Accumulation of clutter can however be associated with one's spending habits. A person who is used to impulse buying will in most of the cases find themselves trapped with clutter. To effectively manage clutter and maintain a well organized home, you have to learn how to say no to clutter before you bring them to the home.

Every purchase that you make therefore has to be scrutinized and thought about well before you commit the money to purchase the stuff. You have to decide to end the cycle of accumulation of things and that can be realized by resetting the bad habits into good ones. You can put yourself under some strict discipline by committing to even one month of zero spending on specific stuff that are not adding much value; the things you can easily do without.

Before You Buy Tips

Here are some of the tips that you should consider focusing on before you buy any item in order to stop clutter before it piles.

- Whenever you run out of an item or when any need arises, take time and examine whether it's something that you truly need or if you have something in hand that you can modify to meet the need without having to make a purchase.

- Most of the times people make purchases because they can't locate the same things in the house yet they already have them. By organizing every room and labeling items as shared earlier; you should be aware of where each item is within the house and if not then ensure that you check to confirm availability before making any purchase.

- If you are well organized then you will have a clear insight of what needs to be replaced and what you already have in the house. Avoid clutter by making a list of items that you should buy before walking into the store. Have a grocery list and ensure that you follow your list. If you find it hard o make a list then you should be rest assured that you may be ending up with a few items that may not be necessary.

- If you find the writing of a shopping list to be a challenge then you can set aside the amount of money that you need to spend as you do your shopping. You need to stay disciplined and not take a debit pr credit card to cover for extra items. Just walk into the shop with the knowledge that you will only spend the amount that you have available in your pocket.

- If you find it hard to stay from purchasing extra items whenever you visit a store then you should consider staying away from the store.

Chapter 3

Natural Cleaning Products

Cleaning products helps in keeping the homes free from toxins and chemicals that can be harmful if not attended to. Unlike personal care products and cosmetics that manufactures are mandated to disclose the ingredients used in preparing the products; they are however not mandated to disclose the ingredients used in preparing household products. The lack of foresight in regards to manufacture of household cleaning supplies has created room for manufacture of cleaning products that contain toxic chemicals.

Such chemicals may not be healthy if inhaled or when in contact with the skin. Reading the label alone to ascertain whether the ingredients are suitable or not is not enough, is not enough as some of the labels may have incomplete information. Use of natural cleaning products can save you a lot of money that could be spent on purchasing the cleaning products and they are also healthy to use. If you are to maintain cleanliness in your home then you have to have some insight on how to prepare natural cleaning products.

Having a clean home is vital and use of natural cleaning products helps in mildew and other toxic mold away as such can cause issues if left unattended to. There are natural eco-friendly cleaning products that are available in the market and one can also make homemade cleaning products for use at home. All that one needs to prepare the cleaning products are some essential oils and other environmentally friendly ingredients that have been proven to help with combating some of the tough stains and other hard to clean areas in the home so that they are free of germs.

The dangers associated with common household cleaning products

The fact that you may not physically see the some things doesn't mean that they lack the potential to hurt you. There could be chances of contamination even o the sparkling countertop where you are placing food and dishes on. There are numerous detergents with diverse scents, the task specific cleaners and the bleaches and such can at times cause health hazards which can be either immediate or overtime depending on the types of ingredients used and the composition.

Use of cleaning products that are made from chemicals may lead to cases such as respiratory conditions; irritation of the eyes, burns, asthma and some may even lead to cancer. When using cleaning products, one should also take time and think about the environment and how use of such products may impact the environment. The cleaning products when disposed can also affect the water that we use in the homes. There are also chemicals that are acid based such as some toilet bowl cleaners. Such products can severely burn the skin and if swallowed by mistake, such corrosive products may lead to serious problems. Having knowledge of some of the natural products that you can use in the home is vital. You should however be aware of the ingredients that you are using and should be sure of any form of reactions that mixing the ingredients may cause in the home.

Below are some of the natural products that you can use if you are to ensure that your home is clean and well organized.

All purpose cleaner

This is one of the commonly used cleaning products within the home. All purpose cleaner is suitable for use on the floors, walls, countertops, appliances and multi surface cleaners. These products can be used practically in cleaning almost everywhere within the home. However when choosing all purpose cleaner; extra care should be taken so that you don't end up with those that carry toxic chemicals.

You can however prepare your very own all purpose cleaner by following the steps below;

Ingredients

- White vinegar – ½ c
- Baking soda – 2 tablespoons
- Lavender, lemon or tea tree – 10 drops

Instructions

Mix together vinegar, essential oils and some water together then add baking soda into a clean spray bottle. Fill the bottle up to the top with water then shake gently for the ingredients to mix. You can then spray the surface you intend to clean then wipe with a cloth.

Homemade disinfectant wipes

The ready-made disinfecting wipes are quite vital for eliminating dirt and can be very convenient. Most of the disinfectant wipes can be toxic however those made from natural products are ideal for use. The natural disinfecting wipes can be easily used and disposed and are suitable for cleaning surfaces around the home. Disinfecting surfaces is vital for a clean and healthy household.

Vinegar helps in inhibiting bacterial growth and an effective degreaser with some antibacterial power. Hydrogen peroxide is also another natural disinfectant that's ideal for use in the home.

Here are the ingredients and steps you can follow for making homemade disinfectant wipes;

Ingredients

- Water – 1 cup
- Vinegar – ¼ cup
- Tea tree oil – 8 cups
- Eucalyptus essential oil – 8 drops
- Lemon essential oil – 8 drops
- Empty wipe container –
- 20 squares of cloth

Steps

1. Fold the cloths and place into the empty container then set aside.
2. In a mixing bowl, combine vinegar, water and the essential oils then stir until well combined.
3. Pour the mixture into the tin over the cloths then let them soak in and get ready to pull as you use the wet wipes.

Homemade liquid dish soap

In most of the homes dishes are normally hand washed however there are some home where dish washing machine is used for cleaning the dishes. Use of homemade liquid dish soap helps in limiting exposure to toxins.

Ingredients

- Distilled water – 1 cup
- White distilled vinegar – 1 tablespoon
- Sal suds – ½ cup (Ingredient available in most health food stores)
- Jojoba oil – 1 tablespoon (You can also use other moisturizing oil like olive oil, sweet almond or fractioned coconut oil).

Steps

1. Pour water and vinegar into the soap dispense then shake for the ingredients to combine well.
2. Add sal suds and preferred oil then shake the bottle for the ingredients to combine well.
3. You will then notice bubbles come to the top as you shake the bottle but that's normal.

In order to use, add a few drops of the liquid dish soap to the sponge you're using for cleaning or the dish water and clean the dishes.

Remember to shake the bottle after some days. Sal suds and water are great for making dish soap and the vinegar and oil are actually optional and can still be done away with.

Toilet bowl cleaner

The toilet bowl are normally formulated with an acid that helps in eliminating lime scale, odors, mildew and water stains that are normally found in the toilet bowl. Since the disposed cleaner gets drain to the ground and into the water system, it's advisable that you use brands that are free of bleach and phosphate. There are various ingredients that can be used to prepare natural toilet bowl cleaner and the ingredients can be alternated depending on what's found to be ideal.

Ingredients

- Baking soda – ½ cup
- Citric acid – ½ cup
- Essential oils – 5 drops (lemon, tea tree, lavender or clove) these are great choices as disinfectants and for freshening the air.

Steps

1. Begin by sprinkling all the ingredients around the toilet bowl then allow to stay for about 15 minutes.
2. Scrub the bowl then rinse by flushing.

Glass and mirror cleaner

Glass cleaners are generally made with isopropanol alcohol or ethanol that helps in dissolving grease and grime much faster. I you want streak free mirrors or glasses then you don't have to rinse with water. Ammonia can also be added to the mixture to prevent streaking however the use of ammonium hydroxide in preparing cleaning products can have some health complications since it's an asthmagen that can end up irritating the skin and the eyes. The chemical is also toxic to amphibians and fish.

Ingredients

- Rubbing isopropyl alcohol – ½ cup
- Distilled water – ½ cup
- White distilled vinegar – 1/3 cup
- Lavender - 2 tablespoons

Steps

In a spray bottle, add water, alcohol, vinegar and a few drops of your preferred essential oils then mix well. You can then use the spray cleaner on coffee tables, mirrors, windows and other glass surfaces. A cotton towel can be used for cleaning the mirror and glass surfaces. The cleaner should be stored at room temperature.

Homemade laundry detergent

Laundry detergent is one of the cleaning products that consume a lot of money and knowing how you can prepare your own laundry detergent can be of great benefit and may lead to saving a lot of money. The homemade laundry detergent can either be prepared in liquid or powder form however the below recipe is for the powder form which is easy to prepare and even to store.

Ingredients

- Homemade laundry bar – 1 bar
- Borax – 1 cup
- Washing soda – 1 cup

Steps

Stir the ingredients together in a container until well mixed. You can as well add the mixture in a food processor or a blender for a well combined mixture. Ensure that the mixture settles well before the blender's lid so that you don't end up inhaling the fine particles of the detergent. To use the detergent, you can apply 2 tablespoons for a small load of clothes or 3 tablespoons for heavily soiled clothes.

You can use the ingredients that you are comfortable with and add even some more that you think may enhance the quality of the soap.

Wood floors and furniture cleaner

Wooden surfaces that are within the home require some special treatment in order to ensure that they are well cleaned and conditioned without having to strip away the natural oils in the wood. Most of the wood cleaners are made with artificial dyes, fragrances and some preservatives.

Ingredients

- White vinegar – 1 cup
- Rubbing alcohol – 2 tablespoons (for shine)

- Essential oil – 10 drops (you can use lemon or orange essential oils.
- Distilled water

Steps

Combine all the ingredients in a spray bottle then shake to combine well. Use of essential oils is optional although it enhances the cleaning and creates an appealing fragrance.

Air fresheners

For some people, the hoe cleaning activity is never complete until the room is sprayed with some pleasing aroma. It's however advisable not to use artificial fragrances in the home as they are known to cause allergies, skin irritations, and asthma amongst other conditions. There are air fresheners that also contain ingredients known to damage the respiratory tract and use of such can be a health hazard.

Homemade air fresheners do not only leave a beautiful fragrance in the room but are also safe to use. Smells in some way affect the body chemistry and the brain that's why emphasis should be put in choosing ingredients for preparing the homemade air fresheners.

Ingredients

- Essential oils – 25 drops (sweet orange or wild orange)
- Essential oils – 25 drops lemon
- Essential oil – 12 drops ginger
- Vodka – 2 tablespoons

- Distilled water
- Spray bottle - 4 oz

Steps

Combine all the ingredients into the spray bottle then shake to mix thoroughly until well blended. The ingredients are quite uplifting and also have anti-fungal properties. The lemon also has both antiviral and antibacterial properties.

Chapter 4

Cleaning and Tidying your Home

Once you have succeeded in organizing and decluttering your home; you need to create a clean atmosphere in the home ones everything has been set in its place. You should not only learn about how to clean the home bit also about how you can maintain it into a tidy home. There are also habits that should be adopted in the family if the home is to stay tidy. Cleaning the home is not a fun activity and that explains the reason why many would prefer being in stuffed houses that has clutter all over.

It takes discipline and commitment to clean a house and keep it clean and organized however if one is to sustain the organization and cleanliness in the home then there are things that they should be committed to doing.

Here are some of the house cleaning tips that one should consider following if the homes are to remain organized and clean;

Morning activities

- Ensure that you make your bed as soon as you wake up. This first activity in the morning may help in kick starting your level of productivity and make it much difficult for you to get back to bed.

- Wipe your bedside table every morning. Ensure that you have some quick wipes that you can use for wiping your bedside table.

- Assess your closet as you dress every morning. Keep a bag in your closet where you can throw in the clothing that you no longer need; sort them through once in a month then decide on whether to toss, sell or donate.

Night activities

- Re-hang the items that you wore and avoid throwing clothes on the bed, on the floor or on a chair that is if the clothes can be worn for one more time before taking for laundry. You can also keep dry cleaning items in a different section within your closet.

- Have a dedicated hamper and a laundry basket for each member of the family. You can even use hampers that have two baskets so as to sort the clothing items well in advance.

- Begin a wash cycle immediately you get home if you have sufficient laundry. Avoid keeping unfolded laundry in your bedroom you should instead have a dedicated folding area and be committed to folding clothes and ironing once the drying cycle is done.

Bathroom

- Ensure that you spray your shower with a cleaner after taking a shower. You can give your shower quick cleaning daily, wiping of the surfaces and letting the surfaces rinse.

- Hang your towels on the bars and your robes on the hooks. Your towels should be properly air dry if you are to use them for about two to three times before washing. If you use a bathrobe then having a dedicated hook for the robe in your bathroom will make your home look more like a hotel.

- Keep the laundry hamper for the towels in the bathroom. Don't leave the used towels on the floor or in the tub instead place them in the hamper for laundry.

- Clean the counterparts of clutter as it may not be possible in the mornings. Ensure that you put away items that you used to get prepared in the morning.

- Clean the toilet at night, that time that you need to wash your face and brush your teeth is also the time you can pour the toilet bowl cleaner to soften the stains before you do the scrubbing. Doing the task everyday will ensure that your toilet is spotless clean.

Kitchen

- Empty the dishwasher as you brew your coffee in the morning. The dishwasher should be ready for the breakfast dishes so that the utensils don't end up piling in the sink the entire day.

- If in case you notice a spill of food or coffee, ensure that you clean it right away. Inspect the counter tops and the floors in the morning then clean whenever any stain is identified. Getting cleaning done frequently will easily get you into the habit of cleaning your house as you progress.

- Ensure that you also change the dish towels that you use for wiping dishes. Once your meal is ready, take time and rinse the utensils before settling down to eat. It will become much easier to clean after taking meals.

- Fill and start your dishwasher at night. Don't wait until morning regardless of how tempting it could be to watch some TV instead of doing the dishwasher.

- Wipe the countertops and the cooking surfaces each night before going to bed. Develop the habit of wiping the microwave after each use. You will love the idea of waking up to a clean and spotless kitchen.

Living room

- Keep the baskets in each room then each day walk through the room and fill the basket with clutter that could be lying around in the room. Ensure that you put each item in its place once you are back in the house.

- Wipe the coffee tables and the side tables during the commercial brakes. When watching commercials, ensure that you do some cleaning and organizing of the living room during those commercial breaks like wiping the living room tables.

- Ensure that you fluff your pillows too after use.

Entryway

- Ensure that you keep your bag, coat and the keys in the same spot each morning. Make it easy to get out of the door each morning by having all that you need in the same place before leaving.

- Take out trash when leaving the house and recycle. You can however alternate the days for taking out trash and for recycling but ensure that each morning you engage in either of the activities. The habit helps in preventing garbage from piling in your house.

- Keep the mail sorter in your entry way and you can drop in your mails once you get into the house. You can also empty your tray and pay your bills once in a week.

- Sort out the dirty clothes and store the rest; you don't have to let your gym bag linger all over the place.

Conclusion

Congratulations and thank you for taking your time to read this book all through to the end. I know you have found valuable information in **Home Organizing: Quick Guide on How to Clean, Declutter and Organize Your Room** book. Home organizing is one thing that many people struggle with and managing clutter has been quite a challenge for many people.

As you have read in this guide; you have noticed that deliberate steps and actions must be taken if one is to live in a well organized and clutter free home. The fact that work is involved is something that's causing many people to put up with congested and dirty homes that only lead to more depressing feelings and emotions. Living in a dirty home where you have to comb through clutter every morning to look for stuff like clothing or shoes can be quite stressing.

However this guide has shared valuable insight on how specific rooms can be organized and clutter managed in a way that it no longer becomes a problem. Now that you know what needs to be done to enjoy living in a well organized and clutter free home, go ahead and implement the lessons learnt and see your home become more spacious clean and worth spending every moment in.

I know you have found the book to be valuable; I however have one request. Would you kindly leave a review for this book on Amazon!

Thank you and enjoy organizing your home.

CPSIA information can be obtained
at www.ICGtesting.com
Printed in the USA
LVHW011333260620
659065LV00018BA/1802